WEEKLY 2026 PLANNER & ORGANIZER

I0095628

SLOTH LOVE

NOLA LEE KELSEY

Soggy Nomad Press
Las Vegas, Nevada USA

©2026 Soggy Nomad Press

All rights reserved. No part of this publication may be reproduced, stored in a retrieval system or transmitted in any form or by any means, electronic, mechanical, recording or otherwise without prior written permission from the publisher, except where permitted by law.

ISBN: 978-1-957532-60-8

SoggyNomadPress.com

2026

January

S	M	T	W	T	F	S
				1	2	3
4	5	6	7	8	9	10
11	12	13	14	15	16	17
18	19	20	21	22	23	24
25	26	27	28	29	30	31

February

S	M	T	W	T	F	S
1	2	3	4	5	6	7
8	9	10	11	12	13	14
15	16	17	18	19	20	21
22	23	24	25	26	27	28

March

S	M	T	W	T	F	S
1	2	3	4	5	6	7
8	9	10	11	12	13	14
15	16	17	18	19	20	21
22	23	24	25	26	27	28
29	30	31				

April

S	M	T	W	T	F	S
			1	2	3	4
5	6	7	8	9	10	11
12	13	14	15	16	17	18
19	20	21	22	23	24	25
26	27	28	29	30		

May

S	M	T	W	T	F	S
					1	2
3	4	5	6	7	8	9
10	11	12	13	14	15	16
17	18	19	20	21	22	23
24	25	26	27	28	29	30
31						

June

S	M	T	W	T	F	S
	1	2	3	4	5	6
7	8	9	10	11	12	13
14	15	16	17	18	19	20
21	22	23	24	25	26	27
28	29	30				

July

S	M	T	W	T	F	S
			1	2	3	4
5	6	7	8	9	10	11
12	13	14	15	16	17	18
19	20	21	22	23	24	25
26	27	28	29	30	31	

August

S	M	T	W	T	F	S
						1
2	3	4	5	6	7	8
9	10	11	12	13	14	15
16	17	18	19	20	21	22
23	24	25	26	27	28	29
30	31					

September

S	M	T	W	T	F	S
		1	2	3	4	5
6	7	8	9	10	11	12
13	14	15	16	17	18	19
20	21	22	23	24	25	26
27	28	29	30			

October

S	M	T	W	T	F	S
				1	2	3
4	5	6	7	8	9	10
11	12	13	14	15	16	17
18	19	20	21	22	23	24
25	26	27	28	29	30	31

November

S	M	T	W	T	F	S
1	2	3	4	5	6	7
8	9	10	11	12	13	14
15	16	17	18	19	20	21
22	23	24	25	26	27	28
29	30					

December

S	M	T	W	T	F	S
		1	2	3	4	5
6	7	8	9	10	11	12
13	14	15	16	17	18	19
20	21	22	23	24	25	26
27	28	29	30	31		

JANUARY 2026

SUNDAY 28

MONDAY 29

TUESDAY 30

WEDNESDAY 31

NEW YEARS EVE

THURSDAY 1

NEW YEARS DAY

FRIDAY 2

SATURDAY 3

SHOPPING:

- [ ]
- [ ]
- [ ]
- [ ]
- [ ]
- [ ]
- [ ]
- [ ]
- [ ]
- [ ]
- [ ]
- [ ]

NOTES:

JANUARY

S	M	T	W	T	F	S
				1	2	3
4	5	6	7	8	9	10
11	12	13	14	15	16	17
18	19	20	21	22	23	24
25	26	27	28	29	30	31

January 2026

Sunday 4

Monday 5

Tuesday 6

Wednesday 7

Thursday 8

Friday 9

Saturday 10

Shopping:

- [ ]
- [ ]
- [ ]
- [ ]
- [ ]
- [ ]
- [ ]
- [ ]
- [ ]
- [ ]
- [ ]
- [ ]

Notes:

January

S	M	T	W	T	F	S
				1	2	3
4	5	6	7	8	9	10
11	12	13	14	15	16	17
18	19	20	21	22	23	24
25	26	27	28	29	30	31

JANUARY 2026

SUNDAY 11

MONDAY 12

TUESDAY 13

WEDNESDAY 14

THURSDAY 15

FRIDAY 16

SATURDAY 17

SHOPPING:

NOTES:

JANUARY

S	M	T	W	T	F	S
				1	2	3
4	5	6	7	8	9	10
11	12	13	14	15	16	17
18	19	20	21	22	23	24
25	26	27	28	29	30	31

JANUARY 2026

SUNDAY 18

MONDAY 19

MARTIN LUTHER KING JR. DAY

TUESDAY 20

WEDNESDAY 21

THURSDAY 22

FRIDAY 23

SATURDAY 24

SHOPPING:

- [ ]
- [ ]
- [ ]
- [ ]
- [ ]
- [ ]
- [ ]
- [ ]
- [ ]
- [ ]
- [ ]
- [ ]

NOTES:

JANUARY

S	M	T	W	T	F	S
				1	2	3
4	5	6	7	8	9	10
11	12	13	14	15	16	17
18	19	20	21	22	23	24
25	26	27	28	29	30	31

January 2026

Sunday 25

Monday 26

Tuesday 27

Wednesday 28

Thursday 29

Friday 30

Saturday 31

Shopping:

- [ ]
- [ ]
- [ ]
- [ ]
- [ ]
- [ ]
- [ ]
- [ ]
- [ ]
- [ ]
- [ ]
- [ ]

Notes:

January

S	M	T	W	T	F	S
				1	2	3
4	5	6	7	8	9	10
11	12	13	14	15	16	17
18	19	20	21	22	23	24
25	26	27	28	29	30	31

FEBRUARY 2026

SUNDAY 1

MONDAY 2

TUESDAY 3

WEDNESDAY 4

THURSDAY 5

FRIDAY 6

SATURDAY 7

SHOPPING:

NOTES:

FEBRUARY

S	M	T	W	T	F	S
1	2	3	4	5	6	7
8	9	10	11	12	13	14
15	16	17	18	19	20	21
22	23	24	25	26	27	28

FEBRUARY 2026

SUNDAY 15

MONDAY 16

PRESIDENTS' DAY

TUESDAY 17

WEDNESDAY 18

THURSDAY 19

FRIDAY 20

SATURDAY 21

SHOPPING:

NOTES:

FEBRUARY

S	M	T	W	T	F	S
1	2	3	4	5	6	7
8	9	10	11	12	13	14
15	16	17	18	19	20	21
22	23	24	25	26	27	28

February 2026

Sunday 15

Monday 16

Presidents' Day

Tuesday 17

Wednesday 18

Thursday 19

Friday 20

Saturday 21

Shopping:

- [ ]
- [ ]
- [ ]
- [ ]
- [ ]
- [ ]
- [ ]
- [ ]
- [ ]
- [ ]
- [ ]
- [ ]

Notes:

February

S	M	T	W	T	F	S
1	2	3	4	5	6	7
8	9	10	11	12	13	14
15	16	17	18	19	20	21
22	23	24	25	26	27	28

FEBRUARY 2026

SUNDAY 8

MONDAY 9

TUESDAY 10

WEDNESDAY 11

THURSDAY 12

FRIDAY 13

SATURDAY 14

VALENTINE'S DAY

SHOPPING:

- [ ]
- [ ]
- [ ]
- [ ]
- [ ]
- [ ]
- [ ]
- [ ]
- [ ]
- [ ]
- [ ]
- [ ]

NOTES:

FEBRUARY

S	M	T	W	T	F	S
1	2	3	4	5	6	7
8	9	10	11	12	13	14
15	16	17	18	19	20	21
22	23	24	25	26	27	28

February 2026

Sunday 22
Monday 23
Tuesday 24
Wednesday 25
Thursday 26
Friday 27
Saturday 28

Shopping:

- [ ]
- [ ]
- [ ]
- [ ]
- [ ]
- [ ]
- [ ]
- [ ]
- [ ]
- [ ]
- [ ]
- [ ]

Notes:

February

S	M	T	W	T	F	S
1	2	3	4	5	6	7
8	9	10	11	12	13	14
15	16	17	18	19	20	21
22	23	24	25	26	27	28

March 2026

Sunday 1

Monday 2

Tuesday 3

Wednesday 4

Thursday 5

Friday 6

Saturday 7

Shopping:

- [ ]
- [ ]
- [ ]
- [ ]
- [ ]
- [ ]
- [ ]
- [ ]
- [ ]
- [ ]
- [ ]
- [ ]

Notes:

March

S	M	T	W	T	F	S
1	2	3	4	5	6	7
8	9	10	11	12	13	14
15	16	17	18	19	20	21
22	23	24	25	26	27	28
29	30	31				

March 2026

Sunday 8

Monday 9

Tuesday 10

Wednesday 11

Thursday 12

Friday 13

Saturday 14

Shopping:

- [ ]
- [ ]
- [ ]
- [ ]
- [ ]
- [ ]
- [ ]
- [ ]
- [ ]
- [ ]
- [ ]
- [ ]

Notes:

March

S	M	T	W	T	F	S
1	2	3	4	5	6	7
8	9	10	11	12	13	14
15	16	17	18	19	20	21
22	23	24	25	26	27	28
29	30	31				

MARCH 2026

SUNDAY 15

MONDAY 16

TUESDAY 17

ST. PATRICK'S DAYV

WEDNESDAY 18

THURSDAY 19

FRIDAY 20

SPRING EQUINOX

SATURDAY 21

SHOPPING:

- [ ]
- [ ]
- [ ]
- [ ]
- [ ]
- [ ]
- [ ]
- [ ]
- [ ]
- [ ]
- [ ]
- [ ]

NOTES:

MARCH

S	M	T	W	T	F	S
1	2	3	4	5	6	7
8	9	10	11	12	13	14
15	16	17	18	19	20	21
22	23	24	25	26	27	28
29	30	31				

MARCH 2026

SUNDAY 22

MONDAY 23

TUESDAY 24

WEDNESDAY 25

THURSDAY 26

FRIDAY 27

SATURDAY 28

SHOPPING:

- [ ]
- [ ]
- [ ]
- [ ]
- [ ]
- [ ]
- [ ]
- [ ]
- [ ]
- [ ]
- [ ]
- [ ]

NOTES:

MARCH

S	M	T	W	T	F	S
1	2	3	4	5	6	7
8	9	10	11	12	13	14
15	16	17	18	19	20	21
22	23	24	25	26	27	28
29	30	31				

April 2026

Sunday 29

Monday 30

Tuesday 31

Wednesday 1

Thursday 2

Friday 3

Saturday 4

Shopping:

☐ _____
☐ _____
☐ _____
☐ _____
☐ _____
☐ _____
☐ _____
☐ _____
☐ _____
☐ _____
☐ _____
☐ _____

Notes:

April

S	M	T	W	T	F	S
			1	2	3	4
5	6	7	8	9	10	11
12	13	14	15	16	17	18
19	20	21	22	23	24	25
26	27	28	29	30		

April 2026

Sunday 5

Easter Sunday

Monday 6

Tuesday 7

Wednesday 8

Thursday 9

Friday 10

Saturday 11

Shopping:

- [ ]
- [ ]
- [ ]
- [ ]
- [ ]
- [ ]
- [ ]
- [ ]
- [ ]
- [ ]
- [ ]
- [ ]

Notes:

April

S	M	T	W	T	F	S
			1	2	3	4
5	6	7	8	9	10	11
12	13	14	15	16	17	18
19	20	21	22	23	24	25
26	27	28	29	30		

APRIL 2026

SUNDAY 12

MONDAY 13

TUESDAY 14

WEDNESDAY 15

THURSDAY 16

FRIDAY 17

SATURDAY 18

SHOPPING:

- [ ]
- [ ]
- [ ]
- [ ]
- [ ]
- [ ]
- [ ]
- [ ]
- [ ]
- [ ]
- [ ]
- [ ]

NOTES:

APRIL

S	M	T	W	T	F	S
			1	2	3	4
5	6	7	8	9	10	11
12	13	14	15	16	17	18
19	20	21	22	23	24	25
26	27	28	29	30		

April 2026

Sunday 19

Monday 20

Tuesday 21

Wednesday 22

Earth Day

Thursday 23

Friday 24

Saturday 25

Shopping:

- [ ]
- [ ]
- [ ]
- [ ]
- [ ]
- [ ]
- [ ]
- [ ]
- [ ]
- [ ]
- [ ]
- [ ]

Notes:

April

S	M	T	W	T	F	S
			1	2	3	4
5	6	7	8	9	10	11
12	13	14	15	16	17	18
19	20	21	22	23	24	25
26	27	28	29	30		

April 2026

Sunday 26

Monday 27

Tuesday 28

Wednesday 29

Thursday 30

National Adopt a Shelter Pet Day

Friday 1

Saturday 2

Shopping:

- [ ]
- [ ]
- [ ]
- [ ]
- [ ]
- [ ]
- [ ]
- [ ]
- [ ]
- [ ]
- [ ]
- [ ]

Notes:

April

S	M	T	W	T	F	S
			1	2	3	4
5	6	7	8	9	10	11
12	13	14	15	16	17	18
19	20	21	22	23	24	25
26	27	28	29	30		

MAY 2026

SUNDAY 3

MONDAY 4

TUESDAY 5

CINCO DE MAYO

WEDNESDAY 6

THURSDAY 7

FRIDAY 8

SATURDAY 9

SHOPPING:

- [ ]
- [ ]
- [ ]
- [ ]
- [ ]
- [ ]
- [ ]
- [ ]
- [ ]
- [ ]
- [ ]
- [ ]

NOTES:

MAY

S	M	T	W	T	F	S
					1	2
3	4	5	6	7	8	9
10	11	12	13	14	15	16
17	18	19	20	21	22	23
24	25	26	27	28	29	30
31						

May 2026

Sunday 10

Mother's Day

Monday 11

Tuesday 12

Wednesday 13

Thursday 14

Friday 15

Saturday 16

Shopping:

- [ ]
- [ ]
- [ ]
- [ ]
- [ ]
- [ ]
- [ ]
- [ ]
- [ ]
- [ ]
- [ ]
- [ ]

Notes:

May

S	M	T	W	T	F	S
					1	2
3	4	5	6	7	8	9
10	11	12	13	14	15	16
17	18	19	20	21	22	23
24	25	26	27	28	29	30
31						

May 2026

Sunday 17

Monday 18

Tuesday 19

Wednesday 20

Thursday 21

Friday 22

Saturday 23

Shopping:

- [ ]
- [ ]
- [ ]
- [ ]
- [ ]
- [ ]
- [ ]
- [ ]
- [ ]
- [ ]
- [ ]
- [ ]

Notes:

May

S	M	T	W	T	F	S
					1	2
3	4	5	6	7	8	9
10	11	12	13	14	15	16
17	18	19	20	21	22	23
24	25	26	27	28	29	30
31						

MAY 2026

SUNDAY 24

MONDAY 25

MEMORIAL DAY

TUESDAY 26

WEDNESDAY 27

THURSDAY 28

FRIDAY 29

SATURDAY 30

SHOPPING:

- [ ]
- [ ]
- [ ]
- [ ]
- [ ]
- [ ]
- [ ]
- [ ]
- [ ]
- [ ]
- [ ]
- [ ]

NOTES:

MAY

S	M	T	W	T	F	S
					1	2
3	4	5	6	7	8	9
10	11	12	13	14	15	16
17	18	19	20	21	22	23
24	25	26	27	28	29	30
31						

June 2026

Sunday 31
Monday 1
Tuesday 2
Wednesday 3
Thursday 4
Friday 5
Saturday 6

Shopping:

- [ ]
- [ ]
- [ ]
- [ ]
- [ ]
- [ ]
- [ ]
- [ ]
- [ ]
- [ ]
- [ ]
- [ ]

Notes:

June

S	M	T	W	T	F	S
	1	2	3	4	5	6
7	8	9	10	11	12	13
14	15	16	17	18	19	20
21	22	23	24	25	26	27
28	29	30				

June 2026

Sunday 7

Monday 8

Tuesday 9

Wednesday 10

Thursday 11

Friday 12

Saturday 13

Shopping:

- [ ]
- [ ]
- [ ]
- [ ]
- [ ]
- [ ]
- [ ]
- [ ]
- [ ]
- [ ]
- [ ]
- [ ]

Notes:

June

S	M	T	W	T	F	S
	1	2	3	4	5	6
7	8	9	10	11	12	13
14	15	16	17	18	19	20
21	22	23	24	25	26	27
28	29	30				

UNE 2026

SUNDAY 14

MONDAY 15

TUESDAY 16

WEDNESDAY 17

THURSDAY 18

FRIDAY 19

JUNETEENTH

SATURDAY 20

SHOPPING:

- [ ]
- [ ]
- [ ]
- [ ]
- [ ]
- [ ]
- [ ]
- [ ]
- [ ]
- [ ]
- [ ]
- [ ]

NOTES:

JUNE

S	M	T	W	T	F	S
	1	2	3	4	5	6
7	8	9	10	11	12	13
14	15	16	17	18	19	20
21	22	23	24	25	26	27
28	29	30				

June 2026

Sunday 21

Father's Day & Summer Solstice

Monday 22

Tuesday 23

Wednesday 24

Thursday 25

Friday 26

Saturday 27

Shopping:

- [ ]
- [ ]
- [ ]
- [ ]
- [ ]
- [ ]
- [ ]
- [ ]
- [ ]
- [ ]
- [ ]
- [ ]

Notes:

June

S	M	T	W	T	F	S
	1	2	3	4	5	6
7	8	9	10	11	12	13
14	15	16	17	18	19	20
21	22	23	24	25	26	27
28	29	30				

July 2026

Sunday 28

Monday 29

Tuesday 30

Wednesday 1

Thursday 2

Friday 3

Saturday 4

Independence Dayv

Shopping:

Notes:

July

S	M	T	W	T	F	S
			1	2	3	4
5	6	7	8	9	10	11
12	13	14	15	16	17	18
19	20	21	22	23	24	25
26	27	28	29	30	31	

JULY 2026

SUNDAY 5

MONDAY 6

TUESDAY 7

WEDNESDAY 8

THURSDAY 9

FRIDAY 10

SATURDAY 11

SHOPPING:

NOTES:

JULY

S	M	T	W	T	F	S
			1	2	3	4
5	6	7	8	9	10	11
12	13	14	15	16	17	18
19	20	21	22	23	24	25
26	27	28	29	30	31	

July 2026

Sunday 12

Monday 13

Tuesday 14

Wednesday 15

Thursday 16

Friday 17

Saturday 18

Shopping:

- [ ]
- [ ]
- [ ]
- [ ]
- [ ]
- [ ]
- [ ]
- [ ]
- [ ]
- [ ]
- [ ]
- [ ]

Notes:

July

S	M	T	W	T	F	S
			1	2	3	4
5	6	7	8	9	10	11
12	13	14	15	16	17	18
19	20	21	22	23	24	25
26	27	28	29	30	31	

July 2026

Sunday 19

Monday 20

Tuesday 21

Wednesday 22

Thursday 23

Friday 24

Saturday 25

Shopping:

- [ ]
- [ ]
- [ ]
- [ ]
- [ ]
- [ ]
- [ ]
- [ ]
- [ ]
- [ ]
- [ ]
- [ ]

Notes:

July

S	M	T	W	T	F	S
			1	2	3	4
5	6	7	8	9	10	11
12	13	14	15	16	17	18
19	20	21	22	23	24	25
26	27	28	29	30	31	

JULY 2026

SUNDAY 26

MONDAY 27

TUESDAY 28

WEDNESDAY 29

THURSDAY 30

FRIDAY 31

SATURDAY 1

SHOPPING:

- [ ]
- [ ]
- [ ]
- [ ]
- [ ]
- [ ]
- [ ]
- [ ]
- [ ]
- [ ]
- [ ]
- [ ]

NOTES:

JULY

S	M	T	W	T	F	S
			1	2	3	4
5	6	7	8	9	10	11
12	13	14	15	16	17	18
19	20	21	22	23	24	25
26	27	28	29	30	31	

AUGUST 2026

SUNDAY 2

MONDAY 3

TUESDAY 4

WEDNESDAY 5

THURSDAY 6

FRIDAY 7

SATURDAY 8

SHOPPING:

- [ ]
- [ ]
- [ ]
- [ ]
- [ ]
- [ ]
- [ ]
- [ ]
- [ ]
- [ ]
- [ ]
- [ ]

NOTES:

AUGUST

S	M	T	W	T	F	S
						1
2	3	4	5	6	7	8
9	10	11	12	13	14	15
16	17	18	19	20	21	22
23	24	25	26	27	28	29
30	31					

AUGUST 2026

SUNDAY 9

MONDAY 10

TUESDAY 11

WEDNESDAY 12

THURSDAY 13

FRIDAY 14

SATURDAY 15

SHOPPING:

- [ ]
- [ ]
- [ ]
- [ ]
- [ ]
- [ ]
- [ ]
- [ ]
- [ ]
- [ ]
- [ ]
- [ ]

NOTES:

AUGUST

S	M	T	W	T	F	S
						1
2	3	4	5	6	7	8
9	10	11	12	13	14	15
16	17	18	19	20	21	22
23	24	25	26	27	28	29
30	31					

AUGUST 2026

SUNDAY 16

MONDAY 17

TUESDAY 18

WEDNESDAY 19

THURSDAY 20

FRIDAY 21

SATURDAY 22

SHOPPING:

NOTES:

AUGUST

S	M	T	W	T	F	S
						1
2	3	4	5	6	7	8
9	10	11	12	13	14	15
16	17	18	19	20	21	22
23	24	25	26	27	28	29
30	31					

AUGUST 2026

SUNDAY 23
MONDAY 24
TUESDAY 25
WEDNESDAY 26 NATIONAL DOG DAY
THURSDAY 27
FRIDAY 28
SATURDAY 29

SHOPPING:

- [ ]
- [ ]
- [ ]
- [ ]
- [ ]
- [ ]
- [ ]
- [ ]
- [ ]
- [ ]
- [ ]
- [ ]

NOTES:

AUGUST

S	M	T	W	T	F	S
						1
2	3	4	5	6	7	8
9	10	11	12	13	14	15
16	17	18	19	20	21	22
23	24	25	26	27	28	29
30	31					

September 2026

Sunday 30

Monday 31

Tuesday 1

Wednesday 2

Thursday 3

Friday 4

Saturday 5

Shopping:

- [ ]
- [ ]
- [ ]
- [ ]
- [ ]
- [ ]
- [ ]
- [ ]
- [ ]
- [ ]
- [ ]
- [ ]

Notes:

September

S	M	T	W	T	F	S
		1	2	3	4	5
6	7	8	9	10	11	12
13	14	15	16	17	18	19
20	21	22	23	24	25	26
27	28	29	30			

September 2026

Sunday 6

Monday 7

Tuesday 8

Wednesday 9

Thursday 10

Friday 11

Saturday 12

Shopping:

- [ ]
- [ ]
- [ ]
- [ ]
- [ ]
- [ ]
- [ ]
- [ ]
- [ ]
- [ ]
- [ ]
- [ ]

Notes:

September

S	M	T	W	T	F	S
		1	2	3	4	5
6	7	8	9	10	11	12
13	14	15	16	17	18	19
20	21	22	23	24	25	26
27	28	29	30			

September 2026

Sunday 13

Monday 14

Tuesday 15

Wednesday 16

Mexican Independence Day

Thursday 17

Friday 18

Saturday 19

Shopping:

- [ ]
- [ ]
- [ ]
- [ ]
- [ ]
- [ ]
- [ ]
- [ ]
- [ ]
- [ ]
- [ ]
- [ ]

Notes:

September

S	M	T	W	T	F	S
		1	2	3	4	5
6	7	8	9	10	11	12
13	14	15	16	17	18	19
20	21	22	23	24	25	26
27	28	29	30			

September 2026

Sunday 20

Monday 21

Tuesday 22

Wednesday 23

Autumnal Equinox

Thursday 24

Friday 25

Saturday 26

Shopping:

Notes:

September

S	M	T	W	T	F	S
		1	2	3	4	5
6	7	8	9	10	11	12
13	14	15	16	17	18	19
20	21	22	23	24	25	26
27	28	29	30			

October 2026

Sunday 27

Monday 28

Tuesday 29

Wednesday 30

Thursday 1

Friday 2

Saturday 3

Shopping:

- [ ]
- [ ]
- [ ]
- [ ]
- [ ]
- [ ]
- [ ]
- [ ]
- [ ]
- [ ]
- [ ]
- [ ]

Notes:

October

S	M	T	W	T	F	S
				1	2	3
4	5	6	7	8	9	10
11	12	13	14	15	16	17
18	19	20	21	22	23	24
25	26	27	28	29	30	31

October 2026

Sunday 4

Monday 5

Tuesday 6

Wednesday 7

Thursday 8

Friday 9

Saturday 10

Shopping:

Notes:

October

S	M	T	W	T	F	S
				1	2	3
4	5	6	7	8	9	10
11	12	13	14	15	16	17
18	19	20	21	22	23	24
25	26	27	28	29	30	31

October 2026

Sunday 11

Monday 12

Tuesday 13

Wednesday 14

Thursday 15

Friday 16

Saturday 17

Shopping:

- [ ]
- [ ]
- [ ]
- [ ]
- [ ]
- [ ]
- [ ]
- [ ]
- [ ]
- [ ]
- [ ]
- [ ]

Notes:

October

S	M	T	W	T	F	S
				1	2	3
4	5	6	7	8	9	10
11	12	13	14	15	16	17
18	19	20	21	22	23	24
25	26	27	28	29	30	31

October 2026

Sunday 18

Monday 19

Tuesday 20

Wednesday 21

Thursday 22

Friday 23

Saturday 24

Shopping:

- [ ]
- [ ]
- [ ]
- [ ]
- [ ]
- [ ]
- [ ]
- [ ]
- [ ]
- [ ]
- [ ]
- [ ]

Notes:

October

S	M	T	W	T	F	S
				1	2	3
4	5	6	7	8	9	10
11	12	13	14	15	16	17
18	19	20	21	22	23	24
25	26	27	28	29	30	31

October 2026

Sunday 25

Monday 26

Tuesday 27

Wednesday 28

Thursday 29

National Cat Day

Friday 30

Saturday 31

Halloween

Shopping:

- [ ]
- [ ]
- [ ]
- [ ]
- [ ]
- [ ]
- [ ]
- [ ]
- [ ]
- [ ]
- [ ]
- [ ]

Notes:

October

S	M	T	W	T	F	S
				1	2	3
4	5	6	7	8	9	10
11	12	13	14	15	16	17
18	19	20	21	22	23	24
25	26	27	28	29	30	31

November 2026

Sunday 1

Dia de los Muertos

Monday 2

Dia de los Muertos

Tuesday 3

Wednesday 4

Thursday 5

Friday 6

Saturday 7

Shopping:

- [ ]
- [ ]
- [ ]
- [ ]
- [ ]
- [ ]
- [ ]
- [ ]
- [ ]
- [ ]
- [ ]
- [ ]

Notes:

November

S	M	T	W	T	F	S
1	2	3	4	5	6	7
8	9	10	11	12	13	14
15	16	17	18	19	20	21
22	23	24	25	26	27	28
29	30					

November 2026

Sunday 8

Monday 9

Tuesday 10

Wednesday 11

Veterens Day

Thursday 12

Friday 13

Saturday 14

Shopping:

- [ ]
- [ ]
- [ ]
- [ ]
- [ ]
- [ ]
- [ ]
- [ ]
- [ ]
- [ ]
- [ ]
- [ ]

Notes:

November

S	M	T	W	T	F	S
1	2	3	4	5	6	7
8	9	10	11	12	13	14
15	16	17	18	19	20	21
22	23	24	25	26	27	28
29	30					

November 2026

Sunday 15

Monday 16

Tuesday 17

Wednesday 18

Thursday 19

Friday 20

Saturday 21

Shopping:

- [ ]
- [ ]
- [ ]
- [ ]
- [ ]
- [ ]
- [ ]
- [ ]
- [ ]
- [ ]
- [ ]
- [ ]

Notes:

November

S	M	T	W	T	F	S
1	2	3	4	5	6	7
8	9	10	11	12	13	14
15	16	17	18	19	20	21
22	23	24	25	26	27	28
29	30					

November 2026

Sunday 22

Monday 23

Tuesday 24

Wednesday 25

Thursday 26

Thanksgiving

Friday 27

Saturday 28

Shopping:

Notes:

November

S	M	T	W	T	F	S
1	2	3	4	5	6	7
8	9	10	11	12	13	14
15	16	17	18	19	20	21
22	23	24	25	26	27	28
29	30					

December 2026

Sunday 29	
Monday 30	
Tuesday 1	
Wednesday 2	
Thursday 3	
Friday 4	
Saturday 5	

Shopping:

- [ ]
- [ ]
- [ ]
- [ ]
- [ ]
- [ ]
- [ ]
- [ ]
- [ ]
- [ ]
- [ ]
- [ ]

Notes:

December

S	M	T	W	T	F	S
		1	2	3	4	5
6	7	8	9	10	11	12
13	14	15	16	17	18	19
20	21	22	23	24	25	26
27	28	29	30	31		

December 2026

Sunday 6
Monday 7
Tuesday 8
Wednesday 9
Thursday 10
Friday 11
Saturday 12

Shopping:

- [ ]
- [ ]
- [ ]
- [ ]
- [ ]
- [ ]
- [ ]
- [ ]
- [ ]
- [ ]
- [ ]
- [ ]

Notes:

December

S	M	T	W	T	F	S
		1	2	3	4	5
6	7	8	9	10	11	12
13	14	15	16	17	18	19
20	21	22	23	24	25	26
27	28	29	30	31		

December 2026

Sunday 13

Monday 14

Tuesday 15

Wednesday 16

Thursday 17

Friday 18

Saturday 19

Shopping:

- [ ]
- [ ]
- [ ]
- [ ]
- [ ]
- [ ]
- [ ]
- [ ]
- [ ]
- [ ]
- [ ]
- [ ]

Notes:

December

S	M	T	W	T	F	S
		1	2	3	4	5
6	7	8	9	10	11	12
13	14	15	16	17	18	19
20	21	22	23	24	25	26
27	28	29	30	31		

December 2026

Sunday 20

Monday 21

Winter Solstice

Tuesday 22

Wednesday 23

Thursday 24

Christmas Eve

Friday 25

Christmas

Saturday 26

Shopping:

- [ ]
- [ ]
- [ ]
- [ ]
- [ ]
- [ ]
- [ ]
- [ ]
- [ ]
- [ ]
- [ ]
- [ ]

Notes:

December

S	M	T	W	T	F	S
		1	2	3	4	5
6	7	8	9	10	11	12
13	14	15	16	17	18	19
20	21	22	23	24	25	26
27	28	29	30	31		

December 2026

Sunday 27

Monday 28

Tuesday 29

Wednesday 30

New Years Eve
Thursday 31

New Years Day
Friday 1

Saturday 2

Shopping:

- [ ]
- [ ]
- [ ]
- [ ]
- [ ]
- [ ]
- [ ]
- [ ]
- [ ]
- [ ]
- [ ]
- [ ]

Notes:

December

S	M	T	W	T	F	S
		1	2	3	4	5
6	7	8	9	10	11	12
13	14	15	16	17	18	19
20	21	22	23	24	25	26
27	28	29	30	31		

January 2026

Sun	Mon	Tue	Wed	Thu	Fri	Sat
				1	2	3
4	5	6	7	8	9	10
11	12	13	14	15	16	17
18	19	20	21	22	23	24
25	26	27	28	29	30	31
		Notes:				

February 2026

Sun	Mon	Tue	Wed	Thu	Fri	Sat
1	2	3	4	5	6	7
8	9	10	11	12	13	14
15	16	17	18	19	20	21
22	23	24	25	26	27	28
		Notes:				

March 2026

Sun	Mon	Tue	Wed	Thu	Fri	Sat
1	2	3	4	5	6	7
8	9	10	11	12	13	14
15	16	17	18	19	20	21
22	23	24	25	26	27	28
29	30	31				
		Notes:				

April 2026

Sun	Mon	Tue	Wed	Thu	Fri	Sat
			1	2	3	4
5	6	7	8	9	10	11
12	13	14	15	16	17	18
19	20	21	22	23	24	25
26	27	28	29	30		
		Notes:				

May 2026

Sun	Mon	Tue	Wed	Thu	Fri	Sat
					1	2
3	4	5	6	7	8	9
10	11	12	13	14	15	16
17	18	19	20	21	22	23
24	25	26	27	28	29	30
31		Notes:				

June 2026

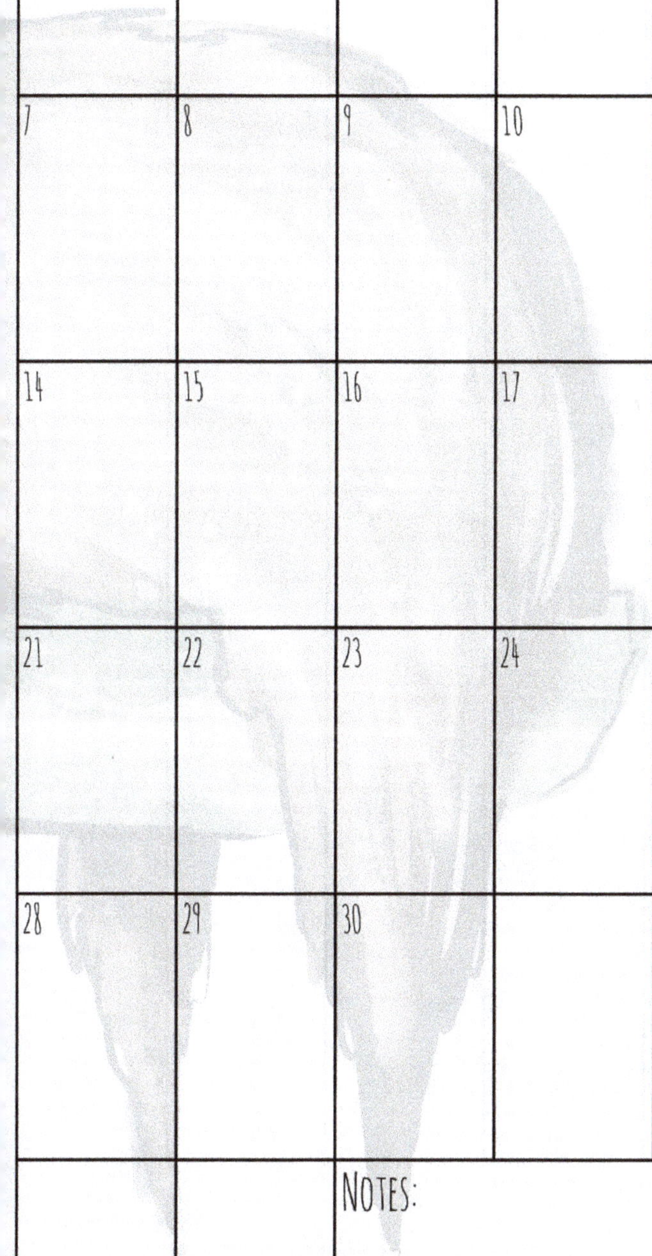

Sun	Mon	Tue	Wed	Thu	Fri	Sat
	1	2	3	4	5	6
7	8	9	10	11	12	13
14	15	16	17	18	19	20
21	22	23	24	25	26	27
28	29	30				
		Notes:				

JULY 2026

SUN	MON	TUE	WED	THU	FRI	SAT
			1	2	3	4
5	6	7	8	9	10	11
12	13	14	15	16	17	18
19	20	21	22	23	24	25
26	27	28	29	30	31	
		NOTES:				

AUGUST 2026

SUN	MON	TUE	WED	THU	FRI	SAT
						1
2	3	4	5	6	7	8
9	10	11	12	13	14	15
16	17	18	19	20	21	22
23	24	25	26	27	28	29
30	31	NOTES:				

September 2026

Sun	Mon	Tue	Wed	Thu	Fri	Sat
		1	2	3	4	5
6	7	8	9	10	11	12
13	14	15	16	17	18	19
20	21	22	23	24	25	26
27	28	29	30			
		Notes:				

October 2026

Sun	Mon	Tue	Wed	Thu	Fri	Sat
				1	2	3
4	5	6	7	8	9	10
11	12	13	14	15	16	17
18	19	20	21	22	23	24
25	26	27	28	29	30	31

Notes:

November 2026

Sun	Mon	Tue	Wed	Thu	Fri	Sat
1	2	3	4	5	6	7
8	9	10	11	12	13	14
15	16	17	18	19	20	21
22	23	24	25	26	27	28
29	30					

Notes:

December 2026

Sun	Mon	Tue	Wed	Thu	Fri	Sat
		1	2	3	4	5
6	7	8	9	10	11	12
13	14	15	16	17	18	19
20	21	22	23	24	25	26
27	28	29	30	31		
		Notes:				

2027

January

S	M	T	W	T	F	S
					1	2
3	4	5	6	7	8	9
10	11	12	13	14	15	16
17	18	19	20	21	22	23
24	25	26	27	28	29	30
31						

February

S	M	T	W	T	F	S
	1	2	3	4	5	6
7	8	9	10	11	12	13
14	15	16	17	18	19	20
21	22	23	24	25	26	27
28						

March

S	M	T	W	T	F	S
	1	2	3	4	5	6
7	8	9	10	11	12	13
14	15	16	17	18	19	20
21	22	23	24	25	26	27
28	29	30	31			

April

S	M	T	W	T	F	S
				1	2	3
4	5	6	7	8	9	10
11	12	13	14	15	16	17
18	19	20	21	22	23	24
25	26	27	28	29	30	

May

S	M	T	W	T	F	S
						1
2	3	4	5	6	7	8
9	10	11	12	13	14	15
16	17	18	19	20	21	22
23	24	25	26	27	28	29
30	31					

June

S	M	T	W	T	F	S
		1	2	3	4	5
6	7	8	9	10	11	12
13	14	15	16	17	18	19
20	21	22	23	24	25	26
27	28	29	30			

July

S	M	T	W	T	F	S
				1	2	3
4	5	6	7	8	9	10
11	12	13	14	15	16	17
18	19	20	21	22	23	24
25	26	27	28	29	30	31

August

S	M	T	W	T	F	S
1	2	3	4	5	6	7
8	9	10	11	12	13	14
15	16	17	18	19	20	21
22	23	24	25	26	27	28
29	30	31				

September

S	M	T	W	T	F	S
			1	2	3	4
5	6	7	8	9	10	11
12	13	14	15	16	17	18
19	20	21	22	23	24	25
26	27	28	29	30		

October

S	M	T	W	T	F	S
					1	2
3	4	5	6	7	8	9
10	11	12	13	14	15	16
17	18	19	20	21	22	23
24	25	26	27	28	29	30
31						

November

S	M	T	W	T	F	S
	1	2	3	4	5	6
7	8	9	10	11	12	13
14	15	16	17	18	19	20
21	22	23	24	25	26	27
28	29	30				

December

S	M	T	W	T	F	S
			1	2	3	4
5	6	7	8	9	10	11
12	13	14	15	16	17	18
19	20	21	22	23	24	25
26	27	28	29	30	31	

2027 Quick Planner

January	February
March	**April**
May	**June**

Notes:

2027 Quick Planner

July	August
September	October
November	December

Notes:

friends an

contacts

CONTACTS

NAME:
PHONE:
EMAIL:
ADDRESS:
NOTES:

NAME:
PHONE:
EMAIL:
ADDRESS:
NOTES:

NAME:
PHONE:
EMAIL:
ADDRESS:
NOTES:

NAME:
PHONE:
EMAIL:
ADDRESS:
NOTES:

NAME:
PHONE:
EMAIL:
ADDRESS:
NOTES:

NAME:
PHONE:
EMAIL:
ADDRESS:
NOTES:

NAME:
PHONE:
EMAIL:
ADDRESS:
NOTES:

NAME:
PHONE:
EMAIL:
ADDRESS:
NOTES:

Contacts

NAME: ______________________
PHONE: ______________________
EMAIL: ______________________
ADDRESS: ______________________
NOTES: ______________________
____

NAME: ______________________
PHONE: ______________________
EMAIL: ______________________
ADDRESS: ______________________
NOTES: ______________________
____

NAME: ______________________
PHONE: ______________________
EMAIL: ______________________
ADDRESS: ______________________
NOTES: ______________________
____

NAME: ______________________
PHONE: ______________________
EMAIL: ______________________
ADDRESS: ______________________
NOTES: ______________________
____

NAME: ______________________
PHONE: ______________________
EMAIL: ______________________
ADDRESS: ______________________
NOTES: ______________________
____

NAME: ______________________
PHONE: ______________________
EMAIL: ______________________
ADDRESS: ______________________
NOTES: ______________________
____

NAME: ______________________
PHONE: ______________________
EMAIL: ______________________
ADDRESS: ______________________
NOTES: ______________________
____

NAME: ______________________
PHONE: ______________________
EMAIL: ______________________
ADDRESS: ______________________
NOTES: ______________________
____

CONTACTS

NAME: ______________________
PHONE: ______________________
EMAIL: ______________________
ADDRESS: ______________________
NOTES: ______________________
____

NAME: ______________________
PHONE: ______________________
EMAIL: ______________________
ADDRESS: ______________________
NOTES: ______________________
____

NAME: ______________________
PHONE: ______________________
EMAIL: ______________________
ADDRESS: ______________________
NOTES: ______________________
____

NAME: ______________________
PHONE: ______________________
EMAIL: ______________________
ADDRESS: ______________________
NOTES: ______________________
____

NAME: ______________________
PHONE: ______________________
EMAIL: ______________________
ADDRESS: ______________________
NOTES: ______________________
____

NAME: ______________________
PHONE: ______________________
EMAIL: ______________________
ADDRESS: ______________________
NOTES: ______________________
____

NAME: ______________________
PHONE: ______________________
EMAIL: ______________________
ADDRESS: ______________________
NOTES: ______________________
____

NAME: ______________________
PHONE: ______________________
EMAIL: ______________________
ADDRESS: ______________________
NOTES: ______________________
____

CONTACTS

NAME:
PHONE:
EMAIL:
ADDRESS:
NOTES:

NAME:
PHONE:
EMAIL:
ADDRESS:
NOTES:

NAME:
PHONE:
EMAIL:
ADDRESS:
NOTES:

NAME:
PHONE:
EMAIL:
ADDRESS:
NOTES:

NAME:
PHONE:
EMAIL:
ADDRESS:
NOTES:

NAME:
PHONE:
EMAIL:
ADDRESS:
NOTES:

NAME:
PHONE:
EMAIL:
ADDRESS:
NOTES:

NAME:
PHONE:
EMAIL:
ADDRESS:
NOTES:

Contacts

NAME: ______________________
PHONE: ______________________
EMAIL: ______________________
ADDRESS: ______________________
NOTES: ______________________
____

NAME: ______________________
PHONE: ______________________
EMAIL: ______________________
ADDRESS: ______________________
NOTES: ______________________
____

NAME: ______________________
PHONE: ______________________
EMAIL: ______________________
ADDRESS: ______________________
NOTES: ______________________
____

NAME: ______________________
PHONE: ______________________
EMAIL: ______________________
ADDRESS: ______________________
NOTES: ______________________
____

NAME: ______________________
PHONE: ______________________
EMAIL: ______________________
ADDRESS: ______________________
NOTES: ______________________
____

NAME: ______________________
PHONE: ______________________
EMAIL: ______________________
ADDRESS: ______________________
NOTES: ______________________
____

NAME: ______________________
PHONE: ______________________
EMAIL: ______________________
ADDRESS: ______________________
NOTES: ______________________
____

NAME: ______________________
PHONE: ______________________
EMAIL: ______________________
ADDRESS: ______________________
NOTES: ______________________
____

Contacts

NAME:
PHONE:
EMAIL:
ADDRESS:
NOTES:

NAME:
PHONE:
EMAIL:
ADDRESS:
NOTES:

NAME:
PHONE:
EMAIL:
ADDRESS:
NOTES:

NAME:
PHONE:
EMAIL:
ADDRESS:
NOTES:

NAME:
PHONE:
EMAIL:
ADDRESS:
NOTES:

NAME:
PHONE:
EMAIL:
ADDRESS:
NOTES:

NAME:
PHONE:
EMAIL:
ADDRESS:
NOTES:

NAME:
PHONE:
EMAIL:
ADDRESS:
NOTES:

Password Tracker

WEBSITE:	USERNAME:
EMAIL:	PASSWORD #1:
PASSWORD #2:	PASSWORD #3:
NOTES:	

WEBSITE:	USERNAME:
EMAIL:	PASSWORD #1:
PASSWORD #2:	PASSWORD #3:
NOTES:	

WEBSITE:	USERNAME:
EMAIL:	PASSWORD #1:
PASSWORD #2:	PASSWORD #3:
NOTES:	

WEBSITE:	USERNAME:
EMAIL:	PASSWORD #1:
PASSWORD #2:	PASSWORD #3:
NOTES:	

WEBSITE:	USERNAME:
EMAIL:	PASSWORD #1:
PASSWORD #2:	PASSWORD #3:
NOTES:	

Password Tracker

WEBSITE:	USERNAME:
EMAIL:	PASSWORD #1:
PASSWORD #2:	PASSWORD #3:
NOTES:	

WEBSITE:	USERNAME:
EMAIL:	PASSWORD #1:
PASSWORD #2:	PASSWORD #3:
NOTES:	

WEBSITE:	USERNAME:
EMAIL:	PASSWORD #1:
PASSWORD #2:	PASSWORD #3:
NOTES:	

WEBSITE:	USERNAME:
EMAIL:	PASSWORD #1:
PASSWORD #2:	PASSWORD #3:
NOTES:	

WEBSITE:	USERNAME:
EMAIL:	PASSWORD #1:
PASSWORD #2:	PASSWORD #3:
NOTES:	

Password Tracker

WEBSITE:	USERNAME:
EMAIL:	PASSWORD #1:
PASSWORD #2:	PASSWORD #3:
NOTES:	

WEBSITE:	USERNAME:
EMAIL:	PASSWORD #1:
PASSWORD #2:	PASSWORD #3:
NOTES:	

WEBSITE:	USERNAME:
EMAIL:	PASSWORD #1:
PASSWORD #2:	PASSWORD #3:
NOTES:	

WEBSITE:	USERNAME:
EMAIL:	PASSWORD #1:
PASSWORD #2:	PASSWORD #3:
NOTES:	

WEBSITE:	USERNAME:
EMAIL:	PASSWORD #1:
PASSWORD #2:	PASSWORD #3:
NOTES:	

NOTES

NOTES

NOTES

NOTES

NOTES

NOTES

NOTES

NOTES

NOTES

SLOTH LOVERS UNITE
ONLINE REVIEWS
SUPPORT SMALL PUBLISHERS
SOGGYNOMADPRESS.COM

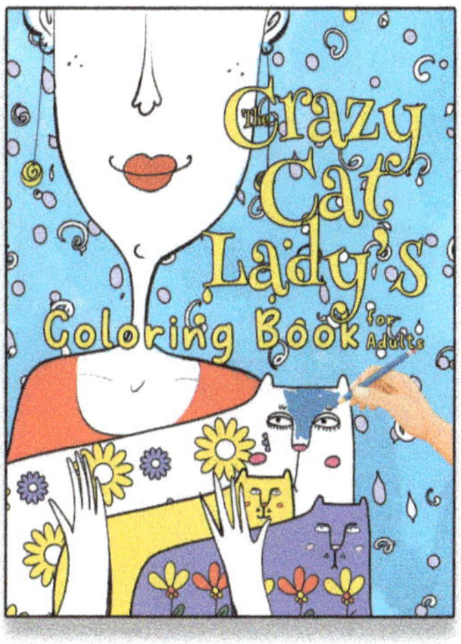

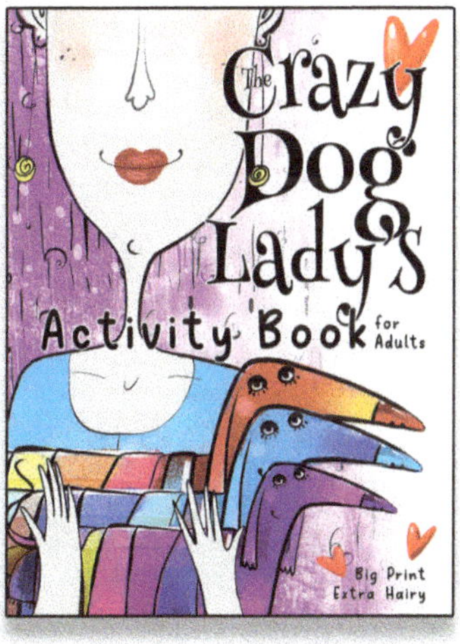

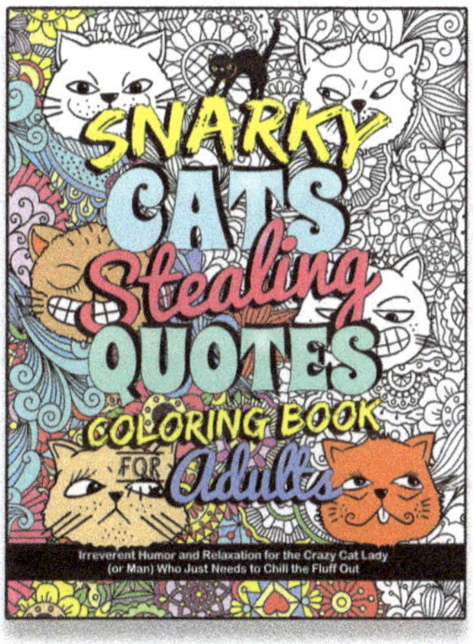

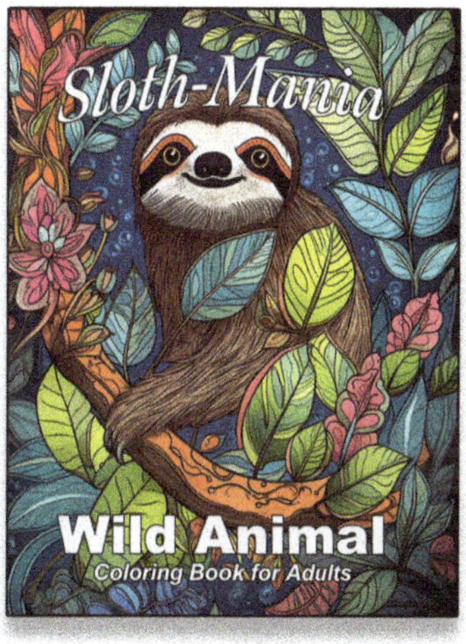

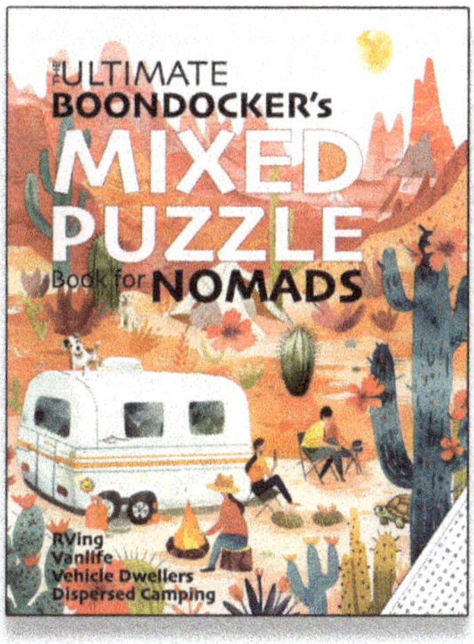

Discover these great books by
Nola Lee Kelsey
www.SoggyNomadPress.com

www.ingramcontent.com/pod-product-compliance
Lightning Source LLC
Chambersburg PA
CBHW052115020426
42335CB00021B/2780